YOUR BOOK IN LIBRARIES WORLDWIDE

SHORT PUBLISHING GUIDES FOR INDIE AUTHORS

ALLIANCE OF INDEPENDENT AUTHORS

CONTENTS

Introduction	v
1. Why Libraries?	1
2. The Opportunity in Ebooks and Audiobooks	5
3. Getting Paid: How Libraries Buy Books	9
4. Preparing Your Approach	15
5. Making Your Approach	23
6. Once Your Book is Stocked	27
7. Other Ways of Earning	31
8. ALLi Members Say	35
9. Summary	39

THE END

Notes	43
Acknowledgments	45
Your Feedback	47
More Advice	49
Alliance of Independent Authors	51

INTRODUCTION

Do you think libraries don't buy books from self-published authors? Think again.

In a 2016 survey conducted by US-based library service New Shelves Books, 92 percent of librarians reported they regularly purchase from self-published authors and small presses.[1] A search of WorldCat, the outward-facing catalogue of the library system, reveals that titles published by KDP (Kindle Direct Publishing), Smashwords, and Ingram (Lightning Source and IngramSpark) are all available in libraries.

Clearly, librarians *are* buying self-published books that fit their acquisitions guidelines.

In chapter one, we discuss this topic in detail but it should be said from the start that although libraries do have a book purchasing budget, and it is possible to get a direct boost in sales, getting your book into libraries is not so much about generating short-term income. Its real value is long-term exposure and discoverability, being found by new readers.

Introduction

Alliance of Independent Authors

This guide to getting your book into libraries is one of the Alliance of Independent Author (ALLi) Quick & Easy guidebooks. These advice guides rely heavily on the group wisdom and experience of ALLi members and advisors.

The advice has usually been published first on our blog, which is written by our members and also draws on discussions in our member forums, and interviews with members and advisors about their inspirations and experiences.

All this advice is generously and freely shared within, and beyond, our non-profit CIC (Community Interest Company) with the intention of paying it forward and benefitting other indie authors.

Our alliance offers many member benefits including: discounts, guidebooks, member forums, contract review, motivation, education, support and more. If you haven't yet, is it time you joined us?

AllianceIndependentAuthors.org

1

WHY LIBRARIES?

As an indie author, you're looking for more readers. What do we talk about when it comes to marketing and driving sales for our books? *Find your readers, reach your readers, go where your readers are.* And who goes to libraries? The most avid of readers.

Your keenest readers are likely to be already in the library.

Does it surprise you to know that Americans, for example, go to the library more often than they go to the movies (1.35 billion visits to the library compared to 1.24 billion movie theater admissions). [1]

According to Pew Research Center, 46 percent of adults ages eighteen and older report visiting a public library or bookmobile in the previous year.[2] And our largest demographic cohort, Millennials, are more likely to have done so than any other generation, using the library not just to borrow, but for discovery.

So if you're looking to reach readers who are mobile and digital, libraries are the best place.

Up to 60 percent of millennials will check a book out of the library and go buy it after, in print or in digital. If you're looking to grow readership, libraries are where readers are.

— ALEXIS PETRIC-BLACK, OVERDRIVE

Petric-Black, in conversation with ALLi at Digital Book World 2019, says when a library buys your book, it's like they're paying you to market your book.

> *Libraries are not going to allow you to retire early, but they will allow you to get money to get income and advertise your book for free. When you think of every single library and they all have a new in this week, new in this month, a librarian pick, you know whenever it comes out, you will be on the front page of a library's website.*

— AMY COLLINS, NEW SHELVES BOOKS

Research by BookNet Canada and reported in 2019 by Porter Anderson in Publishing Perspectives[3] suggests that library patrons buy three times as many books as compared to book buyers who do not visit libraries.

BookNet's research, while specific to Canada, also highlights that the public library is the fourth most popular way readers in general discover new books, especially ebooks and digital audio.

Librarians Love Books — and Authors

Most librarians love or are at least sympathetic to authors. Some are even authors themselves. It's hard to think of another sector where staff think authors are the bee's knees.

That makes librarians significant influencers in the book ecosystem. Even if a library only has one copy of your book, word of mouth and reviews from a librarian cannot be underestimated.

How Many Libraries Are There?

Just as you can find ALLi (Alliance of Independent Authors)

members on all continents, libraries of all kinds are to be found everywhere.

There are 2.5 million[4] national, academic, public, community, school and corporate libraries worldwide and they're an important cultural touchstone for readers and writers alike.

- The US has more than 9,000[5] public libraries.
- Canada has over 3300.
- In South and Central America, examples include Mexico, with 7160 public libraries, Colombia with 1609, Argentina with 1545, and Brazil with 6545.
- On the African continent, South Africa has 1800 public libraries, Morocco has 600, Ghana 257 and Ethiopia 249.
- In the EU, Ireland has 348, Italy 7000, France 3410, Poland 8290, Germany 8195, Switzerland 2000, Belgium 641.
- The UK, at the time of this writing on the brink of Brexit, there are 4100 public libraries.
- China, Russia, India, and Ukraine boast the most public libraries, with 51,311, 46,000; 29,800; and 18,323 respectively. Iran has 3950, Thailand 2116 and the Philippines 1224.
- And finally, at the right-hand side of our map, we have Australia with 1429 public libraries and New Zealand with 296. [6]

How Do Libraries Know About My Book?

As ever, when you want somebody to order your book there are two things you have to consider: distribution and marketing. You need ways for libraries to learn that your book exists, and you need ways to make your books available to library buyers who are interested.

Having good metadata — that's BISAC code, categories, and keywords—of your book is vital to your book's discovery in the library system, as in bookstores.

Book distributors send a metadata feed to its distribution partners (See Chapter 3 Getting Paid: How Libraries Buy Books). A store or library can search for your book and see its metadata. This ensures it appears in relevant searches, but this in itself probably won't be enough to sell your book to a library.

Libraries, like other retailers, can't order a book that they don't already know about. So marketing and promotion activities are as important with libraries as they are anywhere else that you wish to sell your book, or let people know it exists.

2

THE OPPORTUNITY IN EBOOKS AND AUDIOBOOKS

I'm more excited for indie authors in the library market right now than I have been in the last five years because of how badly the standard houses are screwing up.

— AMY COLLINS, NEW SHELVES BOOKS

The funnel into the library market for print books has narrowed for a number of reasons, including a reduction in the number of wholesale distributors, especially in the US. Fewer wholesalers serving libraries means it's harder for author publishers (that's you!) to get print books into libraries. It's far more competitive.

Ebooks and digital audiobooks are an entirely different story. Libraries across the world are responding to digital change and addressing consumer demand for digital books. It's quicker and easier to track sales and lending rates of digital books so, as curating librarians watch what's popular in their communities, they can react quickly to increase their inventory as their budget allows.

Some libraries are reporting a 60 to 80 percent growth rate in eBook and audiobook checkouts in 2019.[1]

But there's more going on to explain the digital opportunity for you to get your self-published book into libraries.

Publisher Embargo

The "Big Five" trade-publishers have for the most part been ambivalent about eBook lending in libraries, in many cases holding back in fear over the ease of copying and piracy. This leaves more room for self-published authors to get in on the eBook action in libraries.

As ALLi News Editor Dan Holloway reported in July 2019, publishers and libraries have long disagreed on the terms on which the former makes ebooks available to the latter. It used to be that libraries could purchase ebooks from a publisher and proceed to lend them out in perpetuity, as often as they could. However, the landscape is changing. Now, many libraries are forced to pay more for popular books. And in one specific case, MacMillan allows a library only a single digital copy for eight weeks after publication, after which they can purchase more copies at a higher price and with metered usage.[2]

> MacMillan insists this is vital to stop libraries eroding the level of royalties their authors receive. Others point out the vital role libraries play in fostering literacy.
>
> — DAN HOLLOWAY, ALLI NEWS EDITOR

The American Library Association and the Public Library Association in the US launched a public campaign against MacMillan's move.

> ALA's goal is to send a clear message to Macmillan's CEO John Sargent: e-book access should be neither denied nor delayed. Our

members are telling us their patrons want an easy way to join this movement and demand e-book access for all. Libraries have millions of allies out there, and we're inviting them to take action.

— ALA EXECUTIVE DIRECTOR MARY GHIKAS

Regardless of how you feel about the issues, it's never been easier for indie authors to get their ebooks into libraries. If traditional publishers like MacMillan make it more difficult for libraries to lend their books, that's a gap that indies are ready, willing, and able to fill.

Going Digital

More and more libraries are curating digital products in addition to their traditional physical copies of books: The majority of library systems offer digital books and digital book products (think eBook and audiobooks).

With Millennial readers driving the demand for digital, we're also seeing other digital access tools — ways for library patrons to "borrow" digital content without necessarily having to step foot into a physical library. Hoopla is one example.

Hoopla, which distributes digital media to libraries, shared some usage stats. Their data comes from delivering digital books, video, music, and more to thousands of public libraries reaching five million patrons. When Hoopla began offering ebooks through its service, one of the surprise best-selling categories was cookbooks. The category wasn't marketed; its continuing popularity is organic.

Hoopla has also noticed that audio in the children's space outperforms in libraries when compared to retail.

Overall, Hoopla has seen huge growth in the home use of audio. Hoopla is rooted in the transactional model (pay per use) but is expanding to usage-metered, perpetual-use, and time-metered models so that content owners and libraries can set up plans that make sense.

ALLIANCE OF INDEPENDENT AUTHORS

— JANE FRIEDMAN, THE HOTSHEET

Audiobooks and ebooks are growth areas. In some systems, audio books comprise nearly 30 percent of a library's budget.

3

GETTING PAID: HOW LIBRARIES BUY BOOKS

Libraries don't buy directly from publishers or authors, but from distributors. So your first step is to get your book into a library vendor catalog, by uploading your titles to the right book distributor.

Unlike bookstores, where purchases are often dictated by a head office, most libraries operate independently of each other. Each library operates its own policy, ordering stock from catalogues or by its chosen book supplier based on its community profile. And each has its own budget to spend as it wants, within broad parameters.

There are four kinds of library: public, academic, school, and special. Each has a different purpose and orders different types of books as follows:

• **Public:** Government-funded local and national libraries serve the general public.

• **Academic:** The college and university library market, although smaller, usually has more money than the public sector to spend on books.

• **School:** With smaller budgets than public or academic libraries, school libraries are important for children's or YA (young adult) writers. In the US, there are only two wholesalers selling into the school market.

They sell library binding (heavy bound) books that hold up to the often rough treatment from school kids. If you're serious about selling to the school library market, you'll need to partner with and pay one of these two wholesalers for the coding and library binding system.

• **Special:** Corporate libraries, usually privately run, are devoted to specific purposes, such as medical or law, with budgets from tiny to huge —significant for niche writers.

It's easy to obtain a list of libraries through your local, regional, or national library association. The next task is to understand which distributor supplies their books. Here is a list of the most important distributors of books to libraries, globally.

- Overdrive for ebooks, audiobooks, and videos is the world's largest library eBook platform, offering a procurement and checkout system for over 40,000 public libraries and schools around the world. Baker & Taylor, now owned by Follett, one of the largest distributors of both digital and print books worldwide to thousands of libraries, publishers and retailers.
- Bibliotheca Bibliotheca's digital lending platform, used by more than 30,000 libraries around the world, is called cloudLibrary. Ebooks are supplied through distributors and publishing platforms. There is minimal curation, mostly for technical aspects.
- James Bennett, library vendor in the Australasian marketplace
- Gardners in the UK, a wholesaler of books, ebooks, music, and film to retailers around the world.

So how do you get your books distributed by these companies and organizations. Indie authors use platforms like Smashwords, PublishDrive, or Draft2Digital to list their books on the library databases from which librarians decide which titles to acquire.

Here are the most library-friendly distributors with global reach which you can access directly as an author-publisher.

- Draft2Digital, distributing ebooks via partnerships with Overdrive and Hoopla
- Findaway Voices' distributing audiobooks to retail and library distribution partners globally.
- IngramSpark, distributes to more than 39,000 retailers and libraries for print and ebooks.
- Kobo Writing Life is a sister company to OverDrive, the largest distributor of ebooks to libraries
- Self-e Library Journal offering access mainly to US libraries, via its PatronsFirst delivery platform. Until recently Self-e was a free platform but is now exploring a paid model.

ALLi Watchdog John Doppler considers these library access services in more detail in *Choosing the Best Self-Publishing Services and Companies* (which, like this guide to libraries and all our guidebooks and contract advice, is free to members of ALLi). In that book he says:

> *It's important for authors to recognize that these services are not like for like. They offer different options depending on territory, career priorities, and marketing strategy. Authors must have a clear sense of what they hope to achieve from their book's availability in a library system and choose accordingly.*
>
> — JOHN DOPPLER, *CHOOSING THE BEST SELF-PUBLISHING SERVICES AND COMPANIES*

There are different distributors in different countries and a little research should uncover the information you need. For example, in Australia ALS Library Services supports authors in submitting books for possible inclusion in their monthly promotional listings to libraries.

Many libraries work with multiple vendor partners, and ALLi's "go wide" best-practice advice applies to the library distributors as well: list your book widely, with as many outlets as possible. If you have time to do only one, Kobo Writing Life's arrangement with Overdrive gives wide access and the highest rates for a single-second the click of a button.

OverDrive is Kobo's sister company, so, by distributing to them through Kobo Writing Life, you will receive the exact rate you would get if you had a direct OverDrive account, (50% of your library list price), but without the added hassle of managing two separate accounts or any aggregator royalty cut.

Amazon and Walmart

Amy Collins from New Shelves Books reports that in the US Walmart and Amazon are in a discount war, each trying to get a bigger share of the library business. While a library can order a book through Baker and Taylor and get a 20 percent discount, that same library could order through Amazon or Walmart and receive a 32 percent discount. Collins says more and more libraries are saving money by buying from discount retail sources.

Wait. Are libraries allowed to buy through discount retailers? Not technically, as most are public entities supported in part or whole by their respective governments. They get around this by working through their Friends of the Library program.

The Friends of the Library programs operate fundraisers throughout the year. They'll raise anywhere from a few hundred to a few thousand dollars, then "donate" that money to the library. Only what's starting to happen is the library, rather than receive the cash, will hand over their wish list to the Friends of the Library, who are then free to go and purchase the books on the wish list at the best price they can find. And yes, that is often via Amazon or Walmart or other discount retailer rather than the usual distribution partner.

How You'll Get Paid

When you do get your book into one or more libraries, you'll get paid through one of two models. OC/OU and CPC.

OC/OU is "one copy, one user" and is the standard library model, mimicking that of physical books. Libraries purchase a single copy and can loan it to one library patron at a time. When one person has your book checked out, no one else can "borrow" the book until the first person has "returned" the digital book. If a library wants to be able to loan the book to more than one person at a time, they'll have to "purchase" another "copy." Payment to authors under the OC/OU model is usually three times the list (retail) price, however it will be a single payment at the time the library purchases your title.

CPC stands for "cost per checkout." This is sometimes referred to as "simultaneous use" and it means libraries can loan the digital book product (eBook or audio) to many readers at the same time. Payment to authors under this model is $1/10^{th}$ the list price per loan. So, your payments will be smaller per reader, but there is the potential for payment with each reader. This model also promises greater exposure for your book, simply because more readers at a time means more people talking and recommending your book to others.

Public Lending Rights (PLR)

> The PLR is the legal right that allows authors and other right holders to receive payment from government to compensate for the free loan of their books by public and other libraries.
>
> — JIM PARKER, COORDINATOR OF THE PLR
> INTERNATIONAL NETWORK

As of 2018, there were thirty-three countries with PLR systems.[1] It's been recognized in the EU since 1992. In 1946, Denmark was the first country to implement a PLR, quickly followed in 1947 and 1954 by Norway and Sweden. I 1973, New Zealand was the first non-European country to set up a PLR system. Australia and Canada followed in 1974 and Israel in 1986. Poland's PLR system is the most recent to begin operating, with the first payments to authors made in 2016.

In most cases, PLR payments do not come out of library budgets, but are funded by regional or national governments. There are a few cases where libraries pay for PLR, for example in the Netherlands, where public libraries are independent entities.

PLR is managed in one of three ways.

1. By a collective management organization, as it in in Spain, Germany, the Netherlands, Lithuania, and Slovakia.

2. Legislated and administered by a government body. This is the case in the UK, where PLR is administered by the British Library.

3. Funded directly by government without underlying legislation. Canada, Israel, and Malta all operate this way.

Different Approaches to PLR Payments

Payments to authors will vary, depending on the country's PLR system and how many times a book is borrowed.

Payment-per-loan approaches are found in Finland, Germany, Malta, the Netherlands and the UK. Payment-per-copy, in which the payments are determined by the number of copies a library holds of the book, is the approach employed in Australia, Canada, and Denmark.

Other PLR approaches match payments to book purchases, such as in France, where in addition to government funding, publishers contribute whenever they sell a book to a library.

To qualify for payment, applicants must apply to register their books, audiobooks, and ebooks. (Non-print material does not qualify for registration in the Irish PLR system.[2])

4

PREPARING YOUR APPROACH

Quality, quality, quality. Those are the top three characteristics your book needs to have in order to increase your chances a library will buy your book.

As with all the other aspects of self-publishing, whether you are doing everything yourself or seeking professional help from service providers, demand the highest possible standards to ensure your books are indistinguishable from those produced by commercial publishers.

Whatever the methods of curation, libraries will be more prepared to take a risk on self-published titles over commercial because the pricing tends to be lower. But pricing won't help you if your book doesn't look professional and credible.

The challenges in the public library space are the same as they are in any other online (or bricks and mortar retailer). The number of new books published every day continues to grow and that means increased competition for space.

You don't get away from that in libraries. There is still a fixed number of jackets you can put on a website, there's still a fixed number of promotional

> things you can do in any given calendar, and so you can't fight that. What you can do is increase your impact in the digital space around marketing. All of those things are incredibly important."
>
> — ALEXIS PETRIC-BLACK, OVERDRIVE

Petric-Black emphasizes what we touched on in Chapter 3, *How Libraries Work:* be sure you're optimizing your metadata and strap lines. And keep in mind that you're now working to attract two rather distinct audiences: your so-called B to C perspective (you, as author, are the B=business, your readers are the C=consumer) and your B to B perspective (you to libraries, which are another B=business). In the case of the libraries, your B to B attraction comes first, and in order to seal the deal you need to demonstrate that you can help the library with *its* B to C efforts, which is all about attracting the reader to the title the library has acquired.

Don't worry, this sounds more convoluted than it is. You don't have to do two separate things. It simply means you want to become persistent about the best practices, which Petric-Black confirms haven't changed in twenty years: quality content, quality cover design appropriate for your genre and the reader, and the metadata and SEO (search engine optimization).

As always, your cover art is important. Enticing descriptions on the side of the dust jacket, or the front and back of the paperback, will encourage more borrows. Sometimes a book is judged by its cover.

> *If there's one thing you can do to spend money on, it's a book cover and it matters in digital too. They say in a book store someone will spend two to three minutes exploring to see if there's a title they want to purchase. With digital it is twenty seconds. So you've got twenty seconds until somebody swipes left! What have you done to capture that twenty seconds?*
>
> — ALEXIS PETRIC-BLACK, OVERDRIVE

ISBN

Before your start, you'll want to ensure your book has an ISBN (International Standard Book Number). Without it, as far as the library system is concerned, your book doesn't exist. The ISBN is a thirteen-digit number which all book databases use to track books. You've likely heard that your eBook doesn't technically require an ISBN. Which is true: unless you want your digital book picked up by libraries and retailers beyond KDP. An ISBN tells a lot about your book, including who the publisher is. If you wish to be identified as the publisher, whether your author name or an "imprint" you choose, you must obtain your own ISBN. Don't simply accept one provided to you, for example by Amazon KDP, unless it is from a publishing services provider you've explicitly agreed to their provision of an ISBN. There are more than 160 ISBN agencies worldwide.[1]

Even with your ISBN, you can't count on walking into a library and having them take your book, not even if you're giving it away. Librarians are happy to get the right books for their readers, but they have constraints on what books they can accept and policies on what they can and cannot buy. The high cost of storage and distribution is a practical limitation, and just as in bookstores, shelf space and time are also limited. Librarians are busy people with little time to read about new books, so it's up to you to identify which librarians would be most likely to buy your book and how to get them interested.

SELL SHEET

Librarians need to believe your book is something their readers will want to read. Before you make an approach, create an information sheet that makes it clear to which readership your book is directed, listing comparable titles.

Do not send any attachment to a library, ever. Most libraries now block them. So create a great sell sheet, and then create a landing page containing your sell sheet as a downloadable document. You could use your own website, or a service like Prolific Works (formerly InstaFreebie) which has a free option, BookFunnel or NetGalley. Key points are a branded professional look and feel, and all the information a librarian or other book distributor needs to make a purchase decision:

Book Title and Subtitle

- Author Name
- Genre
- Format
- ISBN
- Pages
- Price
- Contact Info
- Book Blurb
- Cover Art
- About the Author
- Marketing Approach
- Reviews

Use a professional designer, or, if you're proficient, use design tools like Canva or Adobe.

REVIEWS

Pointing to published consumer and editorial reviews will increase your credibility as an author. Librarians generally rely on vendor lists, where self-published authors rarely appear, or on pre-publication book reviews in trade magazines such as *Publishers Weekly* (USA) and the *Bookseller* (UK), or specific library trade magazines like *Library Journal*, *Booklist*, *Choice*, and *Forecast*.

School Library Journal is an offshoot of *Library Journal* that specializes in children's and YA books. There are also review magazines, online and print, that are specific to genres, such as *RT Book Review* (romance) and *Locus Magazine* (science fiction and fantasy). The librarian who is specifically interested in indie books may consult *IndieReader*.

Kirkus and *PW Select* allow self-publishing authors to pay for a review. This fee doesn't guarantee a good review, and neither is it cheap. Per Kirkus' website, for example, the charge for a 250-word "Traditional

Review" is $425 U.S. and the turnaround time is seven to nine weeks. If you want the review expedited, the cost is $575. *PW Select* is viewed by some librarians as not respectable and not worth the read. (Read more about getting reviews in the ALLi guidebook, *The Indie Author's Guide to Reviewers and Reviews.*)

An alternative to reviews is to run events and build local popularity. If your content has a local link, perhaps because it is set in a nearby locale or contains characters from the area, then definitely use that as a way to garner interest. Librarians like to stock books of local interest so try to ensure they are aware of that aspect of your book when you attempt to place it in your local library. Also, if you're doing any local events, talks, or have some press, TV, or radio coverage coming up, let your local libraries know. Alerting your library in advance will give staff enough time to order your book so they're ready to respond to possible interest from the public.

These two case studies from ALLi members illustrate the value of a local link:

Overall, the Welsh libraries were well down on my list of possible outlets with regard to selling or even stocking my books. I had no idea how it might work, and it was entirely by chance that I walked into my local library and met the head buyer. We enjoyed an informal, unplanned chat.

I left a couple of paperbacks with her, so she could peruse the actual product. By the time I'd driven home and logged on to my email, there was a request that I supply forty-eight books, a dozen copies of each title, and an invitation to be a guest speaker at Conwy Library on World Book Day.

Of course, the fact that these novels are set in well-known Welsh towns and locations has clearly helped my cause, but her very first remark to me was that she loved the covers! Yet more confirmation that people do judge books by their covers.

— NOVELIST JAN RUTH, WRITING IN WALES

Both of my novels are set in Birmingham and, because the setting is integral to each story, I'm eager for the books to reach as many Brummies as possible. I got in touch with the reader development team for Birmingham Libraries and asked if I could tell them about my books.

The reception I got was brilliant. My details went to all the community libraries, and I suddenly found I had a book tour in place! Some library visits were to speak to an existing group, others were specially arranged author events. In all cases I was made extremely welcome by the library staff and met by a group of interested people. Sometimes it was an intimate chat with a small group of readers, other times I spoke for longer to a larger audience. Every time was great fun. Not only did I meet people who were interested in my books—either having read the library copy or keen to buy one from me—but I also got to interact with avid readers and pick their brains about what kind of stories they enjoy, what kind they'd like to read.

I'm looking forward to the visits I still have lined up and hope Birmingham Libraries will be interested in my next book, so I can visit again when it's out.

— KATHARINE D'SOUZA, ENGLISH WRITER

Digital Rights Management (DRM)

Traditionally, mainstream publishers sold print copies to libraries at often five to ten times the consumer retail price. After the book has been borrowed a specific number of times, say twenty or thirty, the book may need replacing and the library must purchase a new copy, again at the inflated price.

Absurdly, this print model has been carried over into the digital age, with Digital Rights Management installed in the ebooks purchased by libraries, which both limits the number of individual checkouts and requires a "copy" to be repurchased after an overall number of loans or a preset period.

> — JOHN DOPPLER, IN CHOOSING THE BEST SELF-PUBLISHING SERVICES

Let's talk for a moment about DRM from the readers' perspective. With DRM 'installed' (usually opted into or out of via a check-box when you're setting your book up for distribution with Amazon KDP, Ingram Spark, and others), the reader does not own the ebooks they have purchased. Instead, they have access that can be turned off at any moment. This matters to readers. Ask anyone who has tried to upload music discs to iTunes (puts hand up). Despite owning the discs, at each subsequent software update, more and more of "my" music disappeared from my iTunes account as DRM had been employed. I could not prove digital ownership over the files, despite the fact I'd uploaded them myself.

> If we want people to own the books they buy, we need to make sure they have a file that cannot be taken back and will not stop being supported. That means no third-party DRM. And it means non-proprietary formats. Epub, for example, is a format that W3C has committed to ensuring will work so long as there is an internet. File format and platform matters. I would encourage anyone to familiarize themselves with ALLi's Self-publishing 3.0. Being in full control of what you sell, how you sell, and where you sell is at the heart of it.
>
> — DAN HOLLOWAY, ALLI NEWS EDITOR

> Now is the perfect time to approach libraries with a lifetime access to your book.
>
> — AMY COLLINS, NEW SHELVES BOOKS

Partly because of the actions of trade publishers like MacMillan, embargoing eBook purchase by libraries for at least eight weeks after publication, and many other publishers pricing ebooks at $15 to $18USD.

> There are 9,833 public libraries in the United States alone. So what if they have lifetime? That's 9,000 copies of your book. Think of all the new readers!
>
> — AMY COLLINS, NEW SHELVES BOOKS

Offering your much more reasonably priced eBook to libraries with lifetime access (no DRM), from the perspective of gaining exposure to new readers, simply makes sense.

5

MAKING YOUR APPROACH

Even if your book is listed with one of the distributors mentioned in Chapter 3, *How Libraries Work*, that doesn't necessarily mean it's available for library patrons to discover. Libraries won't typically invest in a book unless there are signs of demand, or another good reason to purchase.

To make the most of the opportunities libraries offer, you must the librarians aware of your book and its merits.

Dust down your library card, stop by, and introduce yourself. The librarian who purchases books is usually the acquisitions librarian or the person in charge of the collection development.

Sometimes there are several, each with responsibilities for specific categories. The person who acquires travel books, for example, may be different from the person who acquires literature or genre fiction.

Check the library's website. If yours is a children's book, the person you want is likely to be head of the children's department or youth services. Each library may have a collection development policy that gives a broad outline of what it collects and whether it buys books or has them donated.

When contacting libraries directly you'll want answers to two questions:

1. Who are the primary decision-makers?
2. Where do these libraries go to purchase their books?

Once you have determined who and how to contact your local libraries (and beyond) you might take advantage of timing as well.

Libraries can and do acquire titles year-round, but they make major purchases during their fiscal year end/fiscal year begin. This time can vary, but for many this is between April and July. This is a good time to approach librarians because they will be spending both remaining and new funds.

Discover what books the library buys and talk to the librarians about how they make purchases, their time frames, and so on.

Some libraries have special systems or sections specifically for self-published local authors. Be conscious that you're building relationships in the same way you are when you approach bookshops to stock your book. As always, be polite, professional, and respectful. Call, email, or set up a brief meeting to ask about their interest in your book.

Consider talking about the lifetime access we discussed in Chapter 4, *Preparing Your Approach*.

Keep the notion of donating some copies of your books in your back pocket. Yes, donating. Libraries are usually nonprofit organizations and that means they're under funding pressure. They like and need donations.

A lot of libraries prefer two copies of a book or more. Cataloging even a fiction book takes time and effort, and many libraries find it makes more economic sense to have at least two copies.

If pitching your book doesn't work, ask about staging an event. Or, find another way you can fill a need for them. An event is a great way to get into your local library, become acquainted with the staff, and meet local readers. Many libraries also have reading groups that might love to have you visit as a guest author.

I did a children's event at my local library, which was a good way to get exposure. I recently discovered that one of my books subsequently had seventy-two library borrows, thanks just to that visit.

— KAREN INGLIS, CHILDREN'S AUTHOR

6

ONCE YOUR BOOK IS STOCKED

Once you've made initial sales to a few local libraries, it's much easier to sell to others and to different kinds of libraries too, so don't stop at your first success story. Expand your territory.

If your book is borrowed regularly, the librarian may be happy to pay for additional copies. If seldom or never borrowed, your book may not last. How long a book stays on the "shelf" depends on the library's available space, how often the book is checked out, and, for physical books, also on the book's condition. Books last longer at central libraries that have a larger and more comprehensive collection; branches are smaller buildings, and their collections are supposed to be popular. That is what they're for, bringing popular books to the general public. So, books, especially novels, tend to be weeded out from branch libraries after a year or so if they're not circulating. This is why you sometimes see libraries selling off physical books that are apparently still in good condition: there haven't been enough loans to justify giving them digital or physical shelf space.

While the real opportunity lies with digital book products, like ebooks and audiobooks, when libraries do stock physical books from indie authors, know that paperbacks circulate better than hardcovers, and hardcovers with dust jackets better than hardcovers without.

SHARE YOUR MARKETING PLANS

Let the librarians know about all the marketing you are doing, including email promotions and in-store events. The library wants to know that the author is heavily invested in the book's success.

If your library has any kind of book blog or feature on its website, offer to contribute, or have someone post a review or make a book recommendation. If you have local fans, encourage them to get involved. Urge local social media followers and email-list subscribers to ask about your book next time they are in the library, perhaps offering some kind of incentive.

Libraries usually take such requests seriously, but they are also well trained in detecting when requests are genuine. So, don't ring up pretending to be a reader. Ask people who have a genuine enthusiasm for your book to make the request. Be an ethical author.

If you hadn't already offered to hold an event before the library agreed to stock your book, do so now, whether for the general public or as part of one of their regular book groups or reading groups.

> Don't confine yourself to purely promotional events. Find out what kind of thing the library would like to provide for users and work out what you could offer to help them. My local council area runs an annual Discover Festival for people to do new things or learn new skills, where I ran a workshop.
>
> — ALI BACON, SCOTTISH NOVELIST

Teaming up with other authors to provide a joint event can add appeal to your local library. Ali Bacon joined forces with the nine other authors in the writers' cooperative Bristol Women Writers to produce *Unchained*, an anthology of their short stories and poems, published to mark Bristol Central Library's 400th anniversary. Launched as part of the Bristol Literature Festival 2013, it led to a writing workshop as part of the Bristol 400 program.

Our group now has a much higher profile, and Bristol Libraries welcome our suggestions for events and activities. It has also given me exposure over a wider area than before and has given all of us enriched networking opportunities with other writing groups, publishers, editors, and performers. The library tie-in was definitely important in catching attention and giving off good vibes—writers and readers all love libraries!

I made the first approach to the libraries, but after a couple of events they started coming to me. I also appeared on local radio during National Libraries Week as a result of library events and contacts. Although I originally offered free copies of my novel, since then the libraries staging events have usually bought copies of whichever book is being promoted."

— ALI BACON

Just like a clerk in a bookstore, librarians are effectively hand selling books. Think of them as ambassadors for your book, quietly but effectively spreading your words to the wider world. Librarians not only help library members find suitable books, they also discuss with each other what they are reading, and therefore books they read and recommend circulate more.

7

OTHER WAYS OF EARNING

If you find the only way to get your book into libraries is to donate copies, don't be downhearted or deterred. There are other ways that you may benefit, financially and otherwise, from having your books stocked there:

• **Exposure:** Your book is being displayed on equal terms alongside trade-published works (and the average borrower will not know the difference).

• **Book discovery:** Borrowers may review and recommend your books, helping you reach more readers.

• **Earnings:** Register for Public Lending Rights (PLR), which accrue from borrows over time. To be eligible for PLR payments, you will need to research whether your country provides this service and then register with the appropriate organization that covers your country's lending system.

Joining your country's equivalent of the Authors' Licensing and Collecting Society (ALCS), if there is one, is also highly recommended. This organization distributes to authors any rights income gained from various uses of published work, such as photocopying. Again, the benefit isn't only financial:

The fees paid out by PLR and ALCS are always welcome. Membership of ALCS and being registered for PLR have both increased my income but I also appreciate knowing how many people are borrowing my books in libraries.

I'm also reassured to know that ALCS—for a lifetime fee of £25 in the UK—will protect and promote the rights of authors writing in all disciplines, ensuring we get fair payment for the various uses of our work.

— LINDA GILLARD

Volunteer Orgs, Associations, Local Businesses

Consider approaching volunteer and community organizations, community organizations, Friends of the Library groups, and local businesses as other means of getting your books into a library — and get paid for them.

You could go to a local business and sell your book at a 50 percent discount. Let's say you had a children's book about teeth. Go to one or more local dentists and talk to her about having twelve copies of your book at a 40 percent discount. The dentist could affix a sticker inside the front saying, "Donated by Dr. Dentist," and those dozen books all get donated to the local library.

Libraries love that stuff. And when books are donated by a local business, libraries aren't as quick to sell them or take them out of circulation when they've been donated by a local business. You do not need to give your book away or donate.

— AMY COLLINS

Working closely and strategically with your local library can clearly help you raise your profile locally and then further afield as your reputation spreads:

> My involvement with libraries has definitely raised my profile locally. Although audiences were fairly modest, some of the events were covered in local papers which also helped spread the word. One press contact came through my local library.
>
> — ALI BACON

8

ALLI MEMBERS SAY

ALLi is a global non-profit association for self-publishing authors, which seeks to foster ethics and excellence in self-publishing. It's founder and director is Orna Ross, whose work with ALLi has seen her named one of the 100 most influential people in publishing (The Bookseller). ALLi members, residing on all seven continents, benefit from solid advice, advocacy for self-publishing authors, free resources, a contract review service, and a number of discounts.[1]

Below are the words of some of those ALLi members who have had experience with the world of libraries.

> A couple of things I have done: When I have received awards or media I announce and add the #libraries #library #librarians (hashtags on social media. Also, once a month I do a search on my book and if I see it in a new library I find them on social media and thank them for adding my book, also adding the above hashtags. I also entered my book in my state's (Washington, US) library book awards, where thankfully it ended up as a finalist (the only indie on the list) which helped get the attention of other libraries.

— MATTHEW D. HUNT

One thing I've noticed on my library network's website is that when you search for a book, it also shows a link to Amazon. So, if the book's not available - or even if it is - the viewer has the option to make a purchase rather than borrow a copy.

— HELEN BAGGOTT

Kobo is owned by Rakuten which also owns Overdrive. When you load your eBook to Kobo, you have an option to add it to Overdrive at that time. Also, you can do the same with Draft2Digital & PublishDrive. From my experience, once it is on Overdrive, the library will show it as "not owned" but if patrons request it the library will often add it.

— D KIRK WALL

I'm speaking only for my experience in the US. I know my books are distributed to libraries around the world through Ingram for print and ebooks through Overdrive, Baker & Taylor, and Bibliotecha. In the US, I have found that most large library systems will NOT automatically take my donated book and stock it. In fact, most will put it in the annual book sales to earn money for other needed services. The only way I've found to consistently get my books in US library systems (without being a bestseller) is to have my fans request it at their library. So far, it hasn't taken a lot of requests either-

-sometimes just one or two people make a difference because it is so rare that patrons actually request a library to stock a book.

In small, community libraries (usually in small towns) my donating a book will make it available there. And I am happy to do it! There is no arrangement for royalties as these small libraries are already very cash strapped.

In terms of ebooks, it is easier for libraries to carry me. Larger systems have a contract that allows them to carry the entire digital catalog (e.g., from Overdrive) but only get charged when a patron selects a copy. Smaller systems carry a curated catalog from Overdrive. In that case, it is up to me to let them know why they want to include my eBook in their catalog. In Oregon, I can tell all of them I am a local author. Sometimes that is enough. Just as with print books, the best way is to ask my fans to request it from their local library.

Though I am distributed also through B&T and Bibliotecha, I don't know the ins and outs of that as all the libraries I've personally spoken with use Overdrive.

As with any move toward discoverability, it helps to also volunteer to do things for the library. For example, many libraries sponsor a variety of literary talks or events. I've been able to get in some libraries by participating in a panel with other authors--talking about the indie publishing experience. I've also volunteered to coordinate a quarterly author library visit where they read from their work, encourage book groups, and answer general questions about writing and publishing. These things are time consuming and they aren't all about just me. If you belong to writer's group, you might see if together they would like to work with libraries in your area to do these kinds of things. It often helps to present your case with a group behind you, with a variety of authors, instead of a single author.

— MAGGIE MCVAY LYNCH

My local library service (UK) buys each new book of mine as they come out - all it took was for a few readers to go in and ask for the first one and now I alert them to a new release. I also have done several talks for the 'Friends of the Library' group, which helps. And I also offered to do workshops for them and have now been asked to do that several times. (And been paid for the privilege.) It's about making connections. Oh, and getting your name / book cover in the local paper at time of release too. The more you can raise your profile, the more likely you are to get into libraries. As for libraries further afield - the key still is to get some folks to request books and they then go on the list for purchase. Trawl your connections and get them to make requests.

— MARGARET SKEA

When I worked in the local library they might buy in something if it was reasonably priced and they felt there would be a demand for it from other readers. The other option would be to get it from another library on an inter-library loan, but as far as I know (a real librarian would know better than me) British Library copies were not involved.

— RUTH DOWNIE

9

SUMMARY

The Pew Research Center reports that a growing number of people believe librarians can help them locate information they can trust....Libraries and librarians empower people to lead with cutting-edge technologies, paths to lifelong learning, and responsiveness to social issues.[1]

— AMERICAN LIBRARY ASSOCIATION, THE STATE OF AMERICAN LIBRARIES 2018

As a self-publishing author, don't overlook the opportunity to have your eBook purchased or placed in a library. The time is right, given the environment, the pricing and positioning strategies of trade publishers, and the digital habits of readers. Getting your digital book product into libraries can bring credible exposure and attention to your work, helping you find new readers which may help you build sales over time.

With 2.5 million libraries worldwide[2], this is a huge sector responding to digital change and consumer demand for ebooks and audiobooks. Getting your book into the hands and minds and devices of as many people as possible is your priority. To that end, let's sum up the top tips for getting your self-published book into libraries:

Quality. Ensure your content is professionally edited and proofread, that your cover is professionally designed, and that you are adhering to current best practices in your book's metadata and SEO.

ISBN. Get one. Without this International Standard Book Number libraries will not accept your book.

Sell Sheet. Create a package letting librarians know what your book is about, who the expected readership is, and to which other well-known titles your book is similar.

Create a landing page with a downloadable sell sheet. Create or hire to create a professional looking and branded sell sheet. Emails with attachments are not an option in this day and age.

DRM. Beware of Digital Rights Management when it comes to your ebooks. ALLi's recommendation is to decline DRM.

Reviews. Aggressively pursue reader and editorial reviews. Keep records of your published reviews and consider whether purchasing a review is a good option for you.

Get to know your local librarians. Find out what types of books they tend to purchase, through which methods they buy, and what time of year they make the majority of their acquisitions.

Share. Let your local librarians know about the marketing plans for your book. You may be able to get involved in events at the library that will help you to further market yourself and your work.

Overall, if you can present a well- designed, professional package of materials, including a downloadable landing page, and you can demonstrate that your book has a good track record, is in demand, through reviews and/or sales, an acquiring librarian will generally give it a fair hearing.

THE END

NOTES

Introduction

1. https://blog.reedsy.com/libraries-self-publishing-authors/

1. Why Libraries?

1. American Library Association, State of America's Libraries Report 2019 http://www.ala.org/news/state-americas-libraries-report-2019
2. Pew Research Center, Retrieved September 17, 2019 from https://www.pewresearch.org/fact-tank/2017/06/21/millennials-are-the-most-likely-generation-of-americans-to-use-public-libraries/
3. https://publishingperspectives.com/2019/05/booknet-canada-study-library-patrons-say-the-buy-books-more-2019/
4. https://librarymap.ifla.org/
5. Source: American Library Association https://libguides.ala.org/librarystatistics/numberoflibrariesovertime
6. https://www.mapsofworld.com/answers/regions/country-public-libraries-world/

2. The Opportunity in Ebooks and Audiobooks

1. 2 https://perspectivesonreading.com/midsized-libraries-are-driving-digital-reading-in-record-numbers/
2. 3 https://www.wsj.com/articles/e-books-make-macmillan-rethink-relationships-with-libraries-11564063800

3. Getting Paid: How Libraries Buy Books

1. https://www.wipo.int/wipo_magazine/en/2018/03/article_0007.html
2. https://www.bl.uk/plr/about-us

4. Preparing Your Approach

1. https://editorialservicce.com/do-you-need-an-isbn

Notes

8. ALLi Members Say

1. www.allianceindependentauthors.org

9. Summary

1. http://www.ala.org/news/sites/ala.org.news/files/content/2018-soal-report-final.pdf
2. https://librarymap.ifla.org/

ACKNOWLEDGMENTS

All good books are a team effort. As well as the author whose name goes on the cover, there's the creative team of editors and designers and formatters who make the book, as well as the distributors and marketers who take it to readers, and the long list of supporters—from family to work colleagues—without whom a book cannot happen.

Then there are the other writers. Everyone who writes a book owes a debt to long line of authors who have gone before. And to all writers, from journalists and academics to storytellers and poets, who publish relevant ideas, information and inspirations that, quite literally, underwrite the book.

As mentioned in the introduction, Alliance of Independent Author (ALLi) guides draw on the wisdom and experience of our members and advisors, freely shared within and beyond our non-profit CIC (Community Interest Company), with the intention of paying it forward and benefitting other indie authors.

For this guide to getting your self-published book into libraries particular thanks are due to John Doppler, who heads the ALLi Watchdog desk, for his detailed scrutiny of online retailers terms and conditions, and to Darren Hardy, UK Manager, Amazon KDP for feedback on Amazon position concerning reviews.

Our thanks to Boni Wagner Stafford and Howard Lovy for editorial and to all the ALLi members and advisors who have contributed experiences and given us permission to quote your work and ideas in this book: thank you for your generosity and for lighting the way for other indie authors.

YOUR FEEDBACK
REVIEW REQUEST

If you enjoyed this book, please consider leaving a brief review on the website where you bought the book.

A good review is very important to our authors and our organisation. Your feedback doesn't have to be long or detailed. Just a sentence saying what you enjoyed.

Please accept our thanks, in advance, if this is something you'd like to do.

MORE ADVICE

We'd love to send you a weekly roundup of self-publishing advice from the ALLi blog.

| Sign up here for an update each Wednesday

Self-publishing tips and tools, news and views, with updates from the Alliance of Independent Authors (ALLi).

ALLIANCE OF INDEPENDENT AUTHORS

THE ALLIANCE OF INDEPENDENT AUTHORS IS THE GLOBAL NON-PROFIT ASSOCIATION FOR SELF-PUBLISHING AUTHORS.

JOIN US FOR RELIABLE ADVICE AND ADVOCACY, TOGETHER WITH MANY MEMBER BENEFITS: DISCOUNTS, GUIDEBOOKS, MEMBER FORUMS, CONTRACT REVIEW, MOTIVATION, EDUCATION, SUPPORT AND MORE.

AllianceIndependentAuthors.org

Your Book in Libraries Worldwide

ebook: 978-1-913349-72-1

Paperback: 978-1-913349-73-8

Large format: 978-1-913349-82-0

© Alliance Independent Authors 2019

All Enquiries: info@allianceindependentauthors.org

❀ Created with Vellum

www.ingramcontent.com/pod-product-compliance
Lightning Source LLC
Chambersburg PA
CBHW071322080526
44587CB00018B/3320